THE HOW AND WHY WONDER BOOK OF
SOUND

Written by
MARTIN L. KEEN

Illustrated by
GEORGE J. ZAFFO

Editorial Production:
DONALD D. WOLF

Edited under the supervision of
Dr. Paul E. Blackwood
Washington, D. C.

Text and illustrations approved by
Oakes A. White, Brooklyn Children's Museum, Brooklyn, New York

GROSSET & DUNLAP · Publishers · NEW YORK

Introduction

The study of sound will lead to one interesting thing after another, as you will quickly discover in this book. What is sound? Why do sounds differ? Why are sounds loud and soft, pleasant or unpleasant, musical or noisy? *The How and Why Wonder Book of Sound* answers these and dozens of other basic questions on this subject.

But perhaps even more interesting than the characteristics of sound are its uses. For example, housekeepers will be pleased to discover that dishes can be washed with sound. There are also ways of recording your heartbeats for careful study by the doctor. As you will read, knowledge of sound has always been put to good use in dozens of ways. Talking and music are but two everyday examples. But with the astonishing development of electricity and electronics, the study of sound has become an even more important science. *Sonar* and *stereophonic* are but two key words that suggest the modern uses of this branch of study.

You will find numerous experiments in *The How and Why Wonder Book of Sound.* They illustrate the basic ideas about sound and they are fun to do. While experimenting, inquiring, investigating and exploring to answer questions about the subject, you will cultivate the very skills needed to become a scientist.

Children, as well as parents and teachers, will find this book a valuable source of information.

Paul E. Blackwood

Dr. Blackwood is a professional employee in the U. S. Office of Education. This book was edited by him in his private capacity and no official support or endorsement by the Office of Education is intended or should be inferred.

Library of Congress Catalog Card Number: 62-9675

Contents

Look at the illustration and try to imagine the world without sound.

Turn off the sound on your TV set and you can better understand what a world without sound would be like.

Sometimes it would be a blessing if there were no sound.

A World Without Sound

We are always surrounded by a sea of sound. There is not a minute of the day when we cannot hear some sound. To get an idea of how big a part sound plays in our lives, imagine what the world would be like without sound. Imagine yourself on a busy street where traffic moves silently. Automobile engines run soundlessly, there is no screech of brakes and an automobile horn never toots. People walk with silent footsteps and close doors noiselessly. Someone drops a few coins which strike the pavement, bounce and roll without the familiar jingling sound. Some workmen unloading a truck drop a crate. It strikes the street and breaks open as noiselessly as if it were only the shadow of a crate. A man whistles to his dog, but the animal still runs about, because no shrill sounds leave his master's lips. You see a friend and call to him, but he continues on his way, because no shout leaps from your mouth.

Many sounds give us pleasure. Almost everyone enjoys music and singing. Think how mournful the world would be if you could not listen to music, nor sing nor whistle when you are happy. On a quiet summer afternoon, the songs of birds, the hum of insects, the rustle of the breeze in the leaves, and perhaps the soft murmur of a brook — all these things give us pleasure, but none of them would exist in a soundless world.

Our safety depends to a large degree on sound. The baby's cry brings his mother quickly to his aid. Everybody recognizes the cry, "Help!" as a signal that someone is in danger. At traffic crossings, the shriek of a train whistle or the blast of an automobile horn warn of approaching danger. Ships in a fog warn of their presence by the croaking of foghorns. In a forest, the cracking sound of a tree about to fall warns the lumberjack to jump out of the way of danger. How difficult it would be to avoid danger in a world without sound.

The most common way mankind communicates thoughts is by talking; that is, by making the sounds we call words. Think how different our lives would be if we could not talk. We could, of course, still communicate with one another by signs, as deaf persons do. But then we would always have to look directly at the person talking to us. We could never talk to someone in the next room nor call to a friend we see on the street. Communicating with large groups would be difficult. A speaker, instead of using a microphone, would probably have his magnified image projected on a large screen, so that the audience could see his hand- and finger-signs. Instead of the telephone for long distance communication, we would probably have some system of blinking colored lights to spell out words in a code. No one would have invented radio, and the first type of broadcasting might have been television — silent television.

Without sound, then, our world would lose some of its beauty. It would be a more dangerous place, and one in which communication would be difficult and cumbersome.

Without sound, we all might have to make use of smoke signals.

The Nature of Sound

What is sound? Sound is a form of energy that is produced by a vibrating object. (Energy is the capacity or ability to do work — to move something — to give it a push or pull.) To vibrate means to move back and forth. The hum given out by a plucked rubber band is due to the

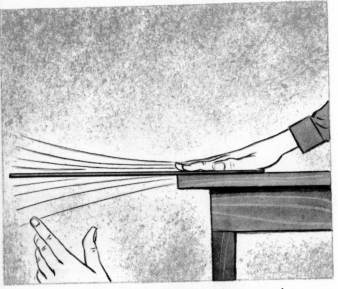
A vibrating object produces sound.

back-and-forth motions of the rubber band. You can easily see the band vibrate; it looks blurry as it moves to and fro. If you strike a fork edgewise on a table, you can see the prongs vibrate at the same time you hear the musical note they give forth. As the prongs vibrate less, the sound dies away.

Firmly hold a ruler, or some other wooden lathe or a nail file on a table so that about two-thirds of the ruler projects over the edge of the table. Then pull downward on the free end of the ruler and suddenly let go. You will see the ruler vibrate up and down at the same time you hear a humming sound.

How can you prove that sound is a form of energy? Obtain a cardboard tube about an inch-and-a-half in diameter. A mailing tube will do very well. If you can't get a mailing tube, roll a sheet of thick paper, about a foot wide, into a tube and fasten it with adhesive tape. Roll a small piece of paper into the shape of a cone and fasten it, too, with adhesive tape. The base of this cone should not be much wider than the diameter of the tube. Fasten the cone to one end of the tube by means of adhesive tape. Now, cut off the tip of the cone, so that you leave a hole a little more than one-fourth of an inch wide.

Cover the other end of the tube with a thin piece of rubber, such as that from a toy balloon. The rubber should be stretched tightly over the end of the tube. Affix the rubber in place with adhesive tape.

Place a lighted candle on a table.

The sound waves will blow out the candle.

Using books, prop the tube in such a position that the hole in the cone points directly at the candle flame. It should also be no more than half an inch from the flame. Be careful not to set the paper on fire!

Now, clap your hands together sharply just behind the tube. The candle flame will suddenly wave about. What moved the flame? Since passage of air through the tube was blocked by the rubber, the flame was not moved simply by wind from your hands moving through the tube. Some form of energy had to pass through the tube to move the flame. This energy was provided by the sound of your hand-clapping.

How do we hear sounds that are far away?

You may wonder how you can hear the back-and-forth movements of a vibrating object. After all, the vibrating object does not touch your ears. You can hear the vibrations because the air conducts the vibrations to your ears.

In its role as a carrier of vibrations between the object and your ears, the air is known as a *medium*. This term comes from the Latin word *medius,* which means "middle." Air serves as a middle, or go-between, to bring the vibrations from the object to your ears.

Air is not the only medium that will conduct sound; other gases will do the same. Liquids and solids are even better conductors of sound. Place a watch on a bare wooden table and press your ear to the other end of the table. You will clearly hear the ticking of the watch. The next time you go swimming, get two stones, put your head under the water and bang the stones together. You will be surprised at how loud a sound the stones make. Ask a friend to stand in the water about 150 feet from you. Let him bang the stones together in the air. Listen to the sound it makes. Then, after you have ducked your head beneath the surface, let your friend bang the stones together in the water. The underwater bang will be much louder, proving that water is a better sound-conducting medium than air.

The watch on the table proved that solids are good conductors of sound. Here is another way you can prove the same thing: With a small nail, punch a hole in the center of the bottom of each of two tin cans. Thread a long, stout string through the holes. Tie a thick knot at each end of the string so that it cannot be pulled through the hole.

Ask a friend to take one can and walk away from you — far enough to stretch the string tight. Place the can over your ear. If your friend now speaks in a low

The string in a tin-can telephone has to be kept taut and should not touch anything.

top of a domed glass container called a bell jar. We place the bell jar on a circular metal plate upon which there is a thin layer of grease. The grease is used to make an airtight seal around the bottom of the bell jar. In the center of the circular metal plate is a hole that leads — through a rubber hose — to a vacuum pump.

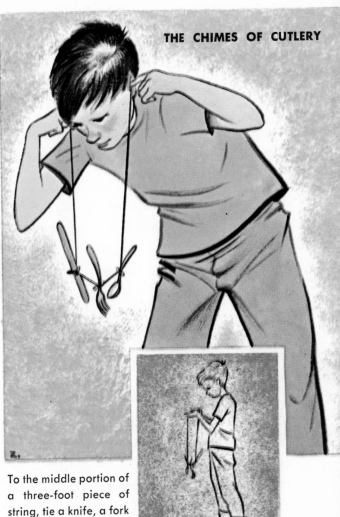

THE CHIMES OF CUTLERY

To the middle portion of a three-foot piece of string, tie a knife, a fork and a spoon about one inch apart. With your fingertips, hold an end of the string in each ear. Let the pieces of silverware swing freely so that they collide with each other. The string will conduct chime-like sounds to your ears. Remove the ends of the string from your ears and note how different the jangling cutlery sounds when air is the conducting medium.

voice into the can at his end, you will hear him clearly. Ask him to remove the can from his mouth and to speak again in the same low voice.

Since you can barely — if at all — hear your friend's voice, then it was the string that conducted the sound of his voice to your ear.

We have just learned that sound travels through a medium — solid, liquid or gaseous. How can we prove that the medium is necessary — that sound would not travel if there were no medium? We tape a pair of small, powerful electric dry-cell batteries to the back of a door bell. Then we connect the batteries to the bell, so that the bell rings.

How can we prove that sound needs a medium to travel through?

With a strong thread, we suspend the bell and batteries upside down from the

9

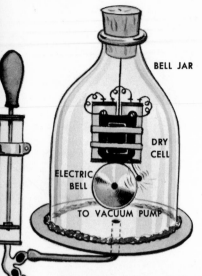

With the experiment described and illustrated below, you can demonstrate the principle that as a vacuum is created, it causes sound to fade. Another experiment might be easier. With a pin and thread, suspend a small bell (or a couple of pieces of metal that can jangle) from the bottom of a cork that tightly fits the mouth of a flask. Heat water in the flask. When the water boils, turn off the heat, and immediately place the cork securely in the mouth of the flask. (Be careful! The neck of the flask will be hot.) When the flask has cooled, shake it, and note how faintly the bell sounds. Steam drove some air from the flask to create a partial vacuum.

We start the pump, which begins to take air out of the bell jar. At first we clearly hear the bell continuing to ring inside the jar. Soon, however, the sound of the bell becomes fainter. As more and more air is removed from the bell jar, the sound continues to become fainter and fainter, until we can no longer hear the bell at all.

What happened to the sound? We can still see the bell ringing, so we know that nothing has happened to the source of the sound. Evidently, something is now missing that formerly conducted the sound of the bell to our ears. Since the air pumped from the bell jar is the only missing item, we can safely conclude it was this air that had conducted the sound of the bell.

If we now let air slowly return through the hose to the bell jar, the ringing reappears and gradually grows louder.

SOUND WAVES

Sound travels through a medium in the form of waves. Let us take sound traveling through air as an example. When a vibrating object, say the prong of a tuning fork, moves in one direction, it pushes the air in front of it. This crowded section of air pushes against the air next to itself, a little farther out from the vibrating prong. The crowding motion that moves farther and farther out from the vibrating object is called a *compression wave*.

What do we mean by compression waves?

While the vibrating prong of a tuning fork compresses the air on one side of itself, it pulls away from the air on the other side and leaves an empty space. The adjacent air begins to rush into this empty space. The place of this inrushing air is taken by the air a little farther out, which, in turn, leaves an empty space behind itself. And the empty space moves outward from the moving prong in the same manner as the compression wave. Although we have said that the space behind the moving prong is empty, actually, it is not entirely without air. Rather, the air in this space is much thinner, or rarer, than air normally is. This zone of rarefied air, moving farther and farther out

What do we mean by rarefaction waves?

from a vibrating object, is called a *rarefaction wave*.

So far, we have told only half the story.

What do we mean by longitudinal waves?

We have seen what happens when the prong of a tuning fork moves in one direction. But a vibrating object moves back and forth. So we must now see what happens when the prong moves in the direction opposite from the one we have been describing. When the prong moves in the opposite direction, it produces a new compression wave in the direction it is moving, and a new rarefaction wave behind itself.

One compression and the following rarefaction (or one rarefaction and the following compression), together, comprise one *sound wave*. Waves of this kind are called *longitudinal* waves. They move outward from a vibrating object like a series of expanding soap bubbles. The bubbles themselves represent the compression waves, and the

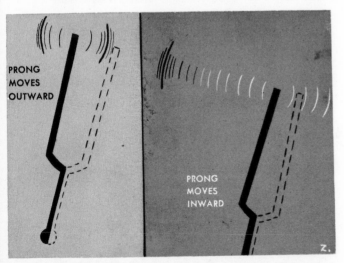

The diagrams illustrate the effect produced by one prong of a vibrating tuning fork. As the prong moves outward, a compression wave starts; as it moves inward, a rarefaction wave starts.

spaces between the bubbles represent the rarefaction waves.

If an object vibrates less than sixteen times a second, it does not produce sound waves, because air particles slip around it, instead of being compressed into waves.

To make some of these facts a little easier to visualize, just imagine

Compression wave: How does it work?

a long train of railroad cars standing on a track. An engine backs against a car at one end of

From a vibrating tuning fork or any other vibrating object, sound waves spread in every direction, each consisting of one compression and one rarefaction.

the train. This pushes the car against the one behind it. The second car pushes against the third, the third against the fourth, and so on. The push imparted by the engine passes along the whole line of cars in much the same way as a compression wave passes through the air — or any other type of sound-con-

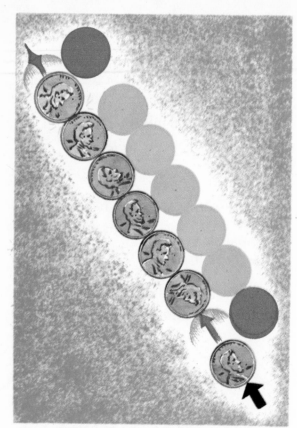

THE COIN THAT GOT AWAY!

On a smooth table, put six coins touching one another in a straight line. Place another coin half an inch directly behind the line. With a flip of your finger, cause this coin to strike the rear of the line. You will see the front coin move forward away from the line. The coin you flip transfers its energy of motion to the line of coins. This energy moves along the line in the form of an impulse that pushes the first coin away from the line.

ducting medium. It is important to note that it is not a railroad car that passes from one end of the line to the other, but rather energy in the form of an impulse. An impulse is a force that starts an object moving. So, the push of the engine is an impulse. Keeping this in mind, you can see that it is not the air next to a vibrating object that moves outward to

The railroad engine, starting to pull the train forward, transmits impulses through the coupling devices. This affects all the other cars in much the same way that a vibrating object produces a rarefaction wave.

form the compression wave; rather, it is energy in the form of an impulse that is transmitted from one section of air to the next.

Now think again of the railroad train

Rarefaction wave: How does it work?

we used as an example of compression. You remember that the engine backed into the line of cars and sent a compression impulse along the whole train. Having attached itself to the train, the engine now moves forward. The coupling devices that hold the cars together are slightly elastic — they have some give in them — so that the whole train does not immediately move forward as a unit behind the engine's first forward pull. Instead, the first car moves forward, leaving a little wider space between itself and the second car. The elastic coupling device then pulls the second car forward, and the original distance between the first two cars is restored. Now, however, the distance between the second and third cars has widened momentarily. This momentary widening passes all along the whole

length of the cars, in much the same way that a rarefaction wave moves through air or some other sound-conducting medium.

Now that we know what sound waves are, we can better understand why the sound of the bell in the bell jar faded away and finally stopped. As the air was pumped from inside the bell jar, there was less and less of a medium in which the vibrating bell could produce compression and rarefaction waves. At last, the air became so thin that the bell could not produce sound waves at all, and we could no longer hear the bell.

Let us take a tuning fork and clamp it firmly to an upright support, so that the prongs are horizontal.

How can we make a vibration write its autograph?

Next, we affix, with sealing wax or some other adhesive, a thin wire or bristle of a brush to the upper surface of one prong, so that the wire projects outward and downward from the end of the prong. We hold a small pane of window glass over a candle flame until the lower surface of the glass is covered by soot.

When the smoked glass has cooled, we place it on some books — the sooty side up. We arrange the height of the books so that the tip of the wire rests lightly on the sooty surface, near one end of the glass. We draw the books along the table straight toward ourselves, so that the end of the wire traces a line in the soot. If we have carefully pulled the books in a straight line, then the line traced by the wire will be straight, too.

Carefully lifting the tip of the wire just a fraction of an inch off the glass, we push the books back to their original position. We release the tip of the wire, and it is now resting on the beginning of the line we have traced. Now, we strike the tuning fork a horizontal blow with a pencil, and again pull the books straight toward us. This time, the tip of the wire traces a wavy line in the soot.

Let us study the lines we have traced. The straight line represents a tuning-fork prong that is not moving. It also represents the point from which a vibrating prong begins its movement in one direction, and to which the moving prong returns before beginning to move in the

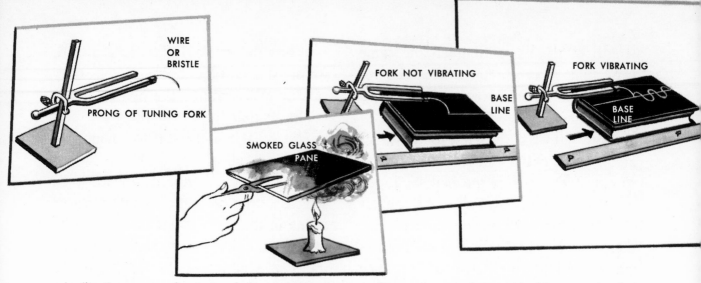

A vibrating prong of a tuning fork writes its autograph. Repeat the experiment with different tuning forks.

opposite direction. As the curved line moves outward from the straight center line, the curve represents a compression. As the curve moves back past the center line, the curve represents a rarefaction. Thus, the wavy line is the autograph of a vibrating tuning-fork prong, and *also* the autograph of a sound wave.

Measuring Sound

One way to measure the speed at which

How fast does sound travel?

sound travels through air is quite simple. Exactly one mile from a group of measuring instruments, a small explosive charge is set off. The light from the explosion travels the intervening mile in 1/186,000 of a second — a time so short that we can ignore it and say that at the same instant the explosion takes place, the flash is recorded by an instrument a mile away. Shortly, another instrument records the sound of the explosion; that is, it records the arrival of the first sound wave from the explosion. The time interval between the recordings of the flash and the sound is the time it takes the sound to travel one mile through air. We find the time to be five seconds. Then in one second, the sound travels one-fifth of a mile.

Scientists have made many measurements of the speed of sound. They have learned that sound travels faster in a warm medium than in a cool medium. For example, at freezing temperature — 32° Fahrenheit — sound travels through air at 1,088 feet per second. At room temperature — 68° F. — the speed of sound through air is 1,129 feet per second. And at 1,800° F., the speed rises to 2,300 feet per second.

Measurements have shown that

sound travels through liquids faster than through air or other gases — and through solids faster than through liquids. For example, sound waves travel through water at room temperature almost 5,000 feet per second — nearly five times as fast as through air. In an iron bar at the same temperature, the speed of sound is more than 16,000 feet per second — fourteen times as fast as through air.

We just learned how the flash and sound of an explosion can be used to measure the speed of sound.

How can you use sound to measure distance?

Now you will learn how you can use a flash of light and accompanying sound to measure distance. We cannot give you an explosive to provide the light and sound, but if you are patient, nature will provide you with these two things, free. All you have to do is to wait for a thunderstorm. The lightning flash and the accompanying thunder are just what you need.

However, before using lightning and thunder to measure distance, let us spend a moment to learn what thunder and lightning are. A bolt of lightning is a giant electric spark leaping between a cloud and the earth, or between two clouds. This huge spark not only sends out a great flash of light, but also a large amount of heat. This heat expands the air surrounding the spark so violently that the air is given a sharp push. As a result, a powerful sound wave travels outward from the zone of heated air. When this wave reaches you, you hear it as a clap of thunder. When lightning flashes nearby, you can clearly detect the powerful sound wave as a single deafening thunderclap. When the lightning is farther away, the sound wave may bounce from cloud to cloud, or from clouds to hills, before it reaches you. As a result of the bouncing, you hear the thunder, not as a single loud clap, but as a series of deep-toned rolling sounds.

The light from a lightning flash reaches you practically instantly, but you have to wait for the sound of the thunder. If you count the seconds between the lightning flash and the first

How can you tell the distance of a lightning flash?

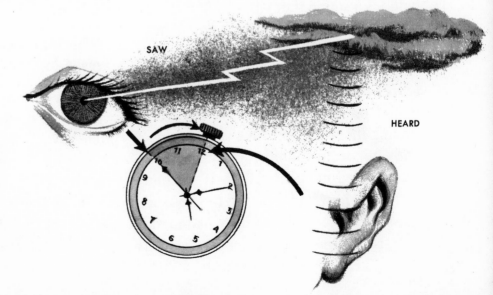

Count the seconds between a lightning flash and the sound of thunder. Then divide this number by five. The answer will tell you how many miles away the lightning struck.

SAW

HEARD

sound of the thunder, and then divide the number of seconds by five, the result will be the approximate distance in miles of the lightning flash. Why? Because at thunderstorm temperature, sound travels in air about one-fifth of a mile a second. If ten seconds elapse between the time you see lightning flash and hear thunder, the lightning is two miles away: 10 divided by 5 equals 2.

When we speak about the "high" or "low" of a sound, we are talking about its *pitch*. A piccolo has a higher pitch than a tuba. The pitch of a canary's chirp is higher than the mooing of a cow. The keys on the right-hand side of a piano have a higher pitch than the keys on the left-hand side.

What is the pitch of a sound?

What is responsible for differences in pitch? Pitch depends on the number of vibrations per second made by a sound-producing object. The number of vibrations per second is called the *frequency* of the sound. The higher the frequency, the higher the pitch.

Scientists speak of frequency in terms of *cycles*. For instance, middle C of a piano is a sound that vibrates 256 times a second, so we say that the frequency of middle C is 256 cycles per second.

We learned that vibrations may be represented by a wavy line, such as we traced on smoked glass. As we were tracing the wavy line, time was passing. Only a certain number of wavy lines were traced in each second. If we had measured how far we moved the smoked glass in one second, and if we had made a mark on the straight line at the end

of each second, we then could have counted the number of wavy lines between each mark. This count would have given us the number of vibrations per second — the *frequency* — of the tuning fork.

Let us make a mark on any part of the wavy line that represents a vibration. Then, we make a mark on the same part of the next wavy line, and so on. The distance between the two marks — as measured on the straight line — is called the *wave length* of the vibration.

If you think about what you have just learned, you will see that the shorter the wave length, the greater the number of vibrations that can take place in a second. In other words, the shorter the wave length, the higher the frequency. Since we know that high frequency results in high pitch, we can now say that short wave length also results in high pitch. We can now also say that notes from a piccolo not only have a high pitch, but also high frequency and short wave length. Notes from a tuba have low pitch, low frequency and long wave length.

Musicians say that persons who can distinguish readily between different pitch have a "good ear," while those who have difficulty in distinguishing pitch have a "poor ear." It is possible to acquire a "good ear" by practice, although for some persons learning this is very difficult. Some persons cannot learn to distinguish different pitches at all and are said to be "tone deaf."

What do musicians mean by "tone deaf"?

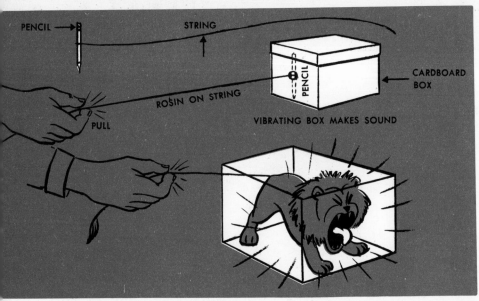

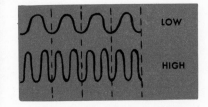

Tie one end of a string about two feet long around the middle of a short pencil. Cut a hole about half an inch across in the center of one side of a cardboard or wooden box. Put the string through the hole so that the pencil is inside the box. Hold the box with one hand. Grip the string between the thumb and forefinger of the other hand, and pull outward, so that the string slips with difficulty through your fingers. From the box will come a lion's roar, a chicken's squawk or a dog's bark, depending on the size of the box and how the string slips through your fingers. The sounds will be greatly increased if you rub plenty of rosin on the string. If you can't get rosin, chalk dust will do. Your fingers slipping along the string cause vibrations that the string transmits to the box, which, in turn, vibrates and magnifies the sound.

Use a compass to draw a circle at least six inches in diameter on a piece of cardboard. Draw another circle with the same center but with a diameter three inches smaller than the first. The inner circle will then have its circumference an inch-and-a-half from that of the larger circle. Cut the larger circle out of the cardboard. Now, cut triangular notches that reach from the outer edge of the circle to the inner circle. This will produce one-and-a-half-inch teeth all around the inner circle.

How can you prove that pitch depends on frequency?

Obtain a hexagonal — six-sided — pencil, sharpened at both ends. Slowly push a point of the pencil through the center of the cardboard disk, until about half the pencil projects on each side.

Make a stand from fairly thick wire. A coat hanger will provide the needed wire. You will probably need a pair of pliers to bend the wire properly.

Place the pencil and cardboard disk on the stand, as shown. Obtain a drinking straw or some other thin tube. Spin the disk with one hand, while blowing air from the straw at the teeth on the disk. (It may be easier to work this experiment with the help of a friend. One of you can turn the disk and the other can direct the stream of air.)

You will note that when the disk is turning fast, the pitch of the sound made by the air striking the disk's teeth will be high. When the disk is turning slower, the pitch will be lower. The stream of air striking one of the moving teeth on the rim of the disk, and then moving past the tooth as the disk turns, causes the air to vibrate fast enough to produce sound waves. The frequency of these vibrations depends on the number

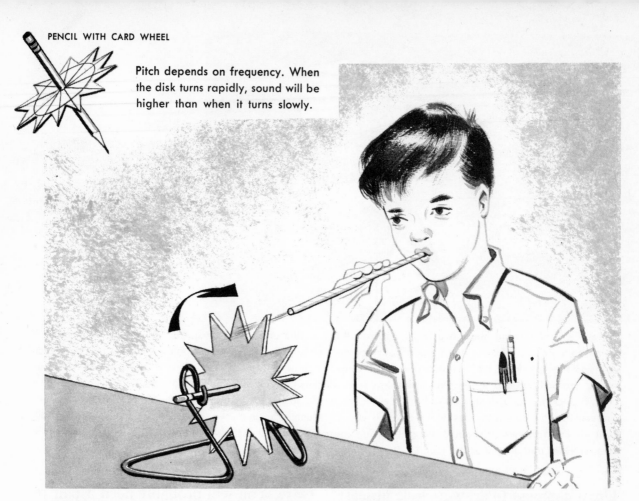

Pitch depends on frequency. When the disk turns rapidly, sound will be higher than when it turns slowly.

of teeth passing in front of the straw. The faster the disk spins, the more teeth pass in front of the straw, and the higher is the pitch of the sound.

Although this experiment clearly shows

How do the scientists give proof that pitch depends on frequency?

that pitch depends on frequency, you will find that the range of pitch is very limited. For this reason, let us see how scientists perform the same experiment with precision equipment. They use a siren — a metal disk with evenly-spaced holes punched in a circle near the disk's rim. A nozzle is fixed so that air passing through it strikes the disk at the point where the holes pass when the disk is turned. Puffs of air passing through the holes give rise to a sound, the frequency

of which is determined by the number of puffs per second. And, of course, the number of puffs per second is determined by the speed at which the disk turns. The frequency of a sound made by a siren can be calculated very easily, if one knows how many turns per second the disk is making. The frequency is equal to the number of turns per second multiplied by the number of holes. For example, if a siren's disk has 36 holes and turns 100 times per second, the frequency of the sound is 3,600 cycles per second.

You may be able to sing a note that has

What is loudness?

exactly the same pitch as a locomotive whistle or a factory whistle, but you surely cannot sing as loud. What determines the loudness of a sound? Loud-

18

ness depends on the amount of energy that goes into making a sound. You know that it is easier to whisper than to shout as loud as you can. When you shout, you put much more energy into making a sound than when you whisper.

If you drop a whole brick on a wooden floor, it will make a louder sound than if you drop only a small piece of the brick. The whole brick strikes the floor with more energy than the small piece. Perhaps you have been near a quarry when a dynamite blast was set off. You not only heard the blast as a loud sound, but you probably seemed to feel a physical blow at the same time. What you felt was a strong compression wave produced by the great energy of the explosion.

Let us examine loudness in terms of our curve tracing on smoked glass. If we have two tuning forks vibrating at the same pitch, they will trace the same number of curved lines in a second of time, because both have the same frequency. But if one tuning fork is louder than the other, how will its curve differ? Its curves will reach farther out from the center line on each side. This means that the prongs of the louder tuning fork move farther back and forth as they vibrate.

The distance the curve moves outward from the center line is called the *amplitude* of the vibration represented by the curve. So, then, louder sounds have waves with greater amplitudes than do softer sounds.

Now, when any object is moved, work is done. And it takes energy to do work. The more the work, the more the energy needed. Therefore, to move the prongs of the louder tuning fork farther requires more energy. Thus, more energy is needed for louder sound.

SIREN

To measure loudness, engineers have

How is loudness measured?

worked out a scale that depends on the amount of energy carried by sound waves. The unit of this loudness scale is the *bel,* named in honor of Alexander Graham Bell, inventor of the telephone. However, sound engineers have found it easier to work with a smaller unit, the *decibel,* which is one-tenth of a bel. Decibels are measured on an instrument, called a *sound-level meter,* that changes sound energy to electrical energy. The sound energy can then be read on the dial of an electric meter. On this meter, zero decibels represents a sound just a little fainter than the human ear can hear, and 100 decibels represent a sound ten billion times as loud.

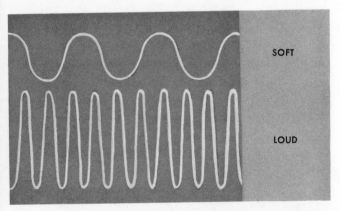

SOFT

LOUD

The higher the top of the wave from the base line on the pane, the louder is the sound. More energy is needed for the louder sound.

Following is a table of the loudness measurements of some familiar sounds:

SOUND	DECIBELS	DESCRIPTION
Thunder	120	Painfully loud
Airplane engine	100-120	Painfully loud
Pneumatic drill	90	Very loud
Heavy traffic	90	Very loud
Hi-fi record player	70	Loud
Ordinary conversation	40-50	Moderate
Quiet home	30	Faint
Whisper	10	Very faint
Rustling of leaves on a tree	10	Very faint

You know that a sound far away is

Why are farther sounds fainter?

fainter than the same sound nearby. The sound of an airplane becomes louder as it approaches overhead, and then fades as the plane flies farther away. So, the farther a sound travels, the fainter it becomes. We have learned enough about sound to understand why loudness fades as sound travels. We know that sound is energy in the form of an impulse that gives particles of air, or other material, a series of motions called waves. We also know that to move anything requires energy, and that energy is used up as the object is moved. The farther a sound wave travels, the more air particles in its path are moved. This means that energy is used up as the sound wave moves along, and the sound

Thread a needle with a piece of thread a foot long. Tie the ends of the thread together. Stick the needle into a small piece of cork. Strike a tuning fork lightly, and place it upright on a table. Suspend the cork so that it just touches the vibrating prong. Note how far the prong moves the cork. Repeat this experiment, striking the tuning fork hard this time. Note how much farther the cork is moved now. When the tuning fork was struck harder, its prongs moved farther back and forth, but they did not move faster. The sound was louder and the waves were stronger.

wave carries less and less energy. Less energy in a sound wave means less loudness. Thus, the farther a sound moves, the fainter it becomes.

Suppose we have two tuning forks of

What is resonance?

the same pitch. We strike one to set it vibrating. The other tuning fork will vibrate, too, even though it is several feet from the first fork. Now, let us repeat this experiment with two tuning forks that do not have the same pitch. What happens this time? The tuning fork we strike fails to cause the other fork to vibrate. Why? Because a tuning fork vibrates with only one frequency — the frequency of its pitch. Sound waves produced by one tuning fork strike the other fork. These sound waves will cause the fork they strike to vibrate only if it has the same pitch as the fork that produces the sound waves. When one object vibrates as a result of regular impulses sent out by another vibrating object, we say that the objects are in *resonance*.

Every object has its own particular

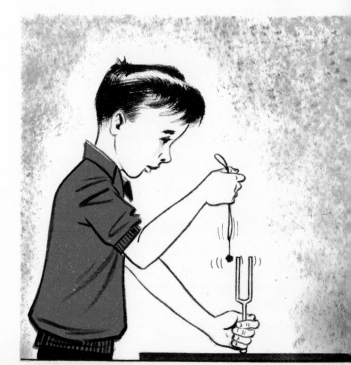

Obtain two empty soda bottles of the same size. Hold one so that its mouth is close to your ear. Ask a friend to stand a few feet from you and to blow strongly across the top of the other bottle until he produces a clear musical tone. When he does this, you will hear the same tone come from your bottle, though more faintly, of course. The vibrations of your friend's bottle caused resonant vibrations in your bottle.

frequency to which it vibrates. This frequency depends mainly on the object's size and shape and the material of which it is made. Perhaps you have been sitting in a quiet room and have heard a window pane suddenly buzz, or some object — maybe a sugar bowl lid or vase — unexpectedly rattle. These objects were vibrating in resonance with sound waves that may have been set in motion by a distant train or truck. The waves then traveled through the ground to your house.

If you have a piano available, you can easily demonstrate how resonance acts. Place a pin, a coin, a pencil or any other small, hard object on the music rack. Beginning at one end of the piano, strike the keys in order. As you pick your way along the keyboard, you will eventually strike a key that will make one of the objects on the music rack vibrate; then another key for another object, and so on. As this happens, each vibrating object is in resonance with the vibrating piano string struck by the key. The striking of some key may cause all the objects to vibrate at once. If this happens, it will be because the piano string is in resonance with the music rack, and the vibrating rack is bouncing the objects up and down.

The Bible tells us that Joshua, the military leader of the ancient Israelis, led an army against the walled city of Jericho. When the army arrived at the city, Joshua commanded it to march around the walls shouting and blowing on trumpets. The great sound made by the army caused the walls to crumble.

How did Joshua win the Battle of Jericho?

It is interesting to let our imaginations play with this story. Picture an army of tens of thousands of marching around Jericho's ranks two-score wide. Thousands of marching feet the ground at the same time foot strikes the ground, its "Ho!" At the same soldiers who have trum splitting blast. What of sound rolls toward the walls! Now, suppose the cadence of the marching feet, the shouts and the trumpets are in resonance with the walls. As the waves of sound strike them, the walls begin to tremble. Dust spurts out from between the great stones as the mortar is powdered by vibrations that strike the walls through the ground and the air. At last, the quaking walls crumble beneath the pounding of the thunderous barrage of sound that beats upon them. Maybe it happened that way.

When soldiers march across a bridge, they are ordered to break step. If they continue to march in step, the frequency of their cadence might be in resonance with the bridge, and this would cause the bridge to tremble violently and possibly collapse. Perhaps you have been at a football game when the spectators in the grandstand began to clap their hands in unison. You not only could hear the clapping, but possibly you

could also feel the grandstand tremble to the cadence of the sound.

Reflected Sound

ound is called an *echo*. In general, an echo has the same characteristics as original sound. If you outdoors and you in the direction of a bluff that is same away, you will back to you. sound the when you

22

spoke it, although it will be fainter, because it lost energy during its round trip.

Most bats eat insects. These insects are caught while flying **Do bats use their eyesight to find insects?** in the dark. How bats are able to locate such tiny prey as mosquitoes and gnats in the dark puzzled men for centuries. In 1793, the

According to the Bible, blasts of sound caused the walls of Jericho to crumble. The illustration is a detail from an engraving by Gustave Doré, the famous French illustrator of the nineteenth century.

to his laboratory, where he dissected their stomachs. He found that the blinded bats had just as many insects in their stomachs as did the bats that could see. From this rather cruel experiment, Spallanzani concluded that bats do not hunt insects by sight and, in fact, do not need light to find their way about.

Spallanzani still did not know how bats catch insects in the dark. To investigate further, he made brass tubes, a twenty-fifth of an inch

How do bats locate insects?

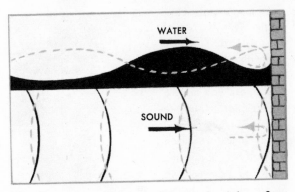

The sound wave of an echo bounces back by reflection, much like water bouncing from a wall.

brilliant Italian scientist Lazzaro Spallanzani became interested in how animals find their prey at night. He learned that owls and certain other night-hunting animals rely on their big eyes to make use of what little light may be available. These creatures became helpless in total darkness. Bats, however, could flit easily through the darkest rooms. Spallanzani blinded some bats. They flew as well as ever. He then put identifying marks on the wings of each bat and released them outdoors. Four days later, he went to the bell tower of the cathedral of Pavia, where he had caught the bats. He climbed into the bell tower at dawn, just when the bats were returning from their night's hunting. He again caught the bats he had blinded. He took them and some others

in diameter. He put these tubes into the ears of bats, and the bats flew about as skillfully as ever. Then he plugged the tiny tubes. Now, the bats flew about clumsily, bumping into every obstacle. Spallanzani concluded that bats somehow used their sense of hearing to locate insects, as well as to fly skillfully among the branches of trees — all in the dark. It was not until nearly one-

and-a-half centuries later that scientists learned how bats perform their marvelous feats of aerial maneuvering.

In 1932, the Dutch zoologist Sven Dijkgraaf found that a faint clicking sound which bats make was connected with the way they locate obstacles. A few years later, the American scientist Donald R. Griffin discovered that bats make a large number of sounds, but all except the faint clicks are of a pitch so high that human beings cannot hear them. Another American scientist, Robert Galambos, showed that covering the mouths of bats, and thereby preventing them from emitting sounds, was just as effective as plugging their ears. This caused them to lose their ability to avoid obstacles when flying in the dark.

Perhaps you have heard bats squeak as they flit about on a summer evening, or perhaps you have heard roosting bats

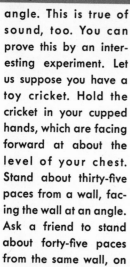

The reflection of sound is much like the reflection of light. When a ray of light strikes a reflecting surface at an angle, the ray is reflected at exactly the same

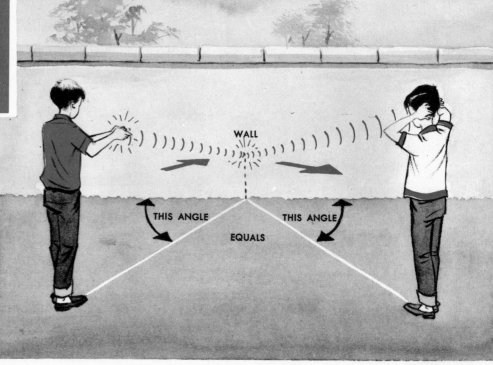

angle. This is true of sound, too. You can prove this by an interesting experiment. Let us suppose you have a toy cricket. Hold the cricket in your cupped hands, which are facing forward at about the level of your chest. Stand about thirty-five paces from a wall, facing the wall at an angle. Ask a friend to stand about forty-five paces from the same wall, on the side toward which you are facing. As you continually click the cricket, ask your friend to walk sideways back and forth, until he finds the place where the clicks sound the loudest. When he finds this place, ask him to cup his hands behind his ears, and then to turn his head back and forth until he finds the position in which the clicks sound the loudest. When he has found this place and position, he should be facing toward a point on the wall midway between you and him. Now, make a mark on the ground right below your cupped hands. Draw a line from this mark to the wall, in the direction toward which your hands were pointing. Ask your friend to draw a line on the ground to the wall, in the direction toward which his nose is pointing. His line should meet the wall at the same point your line did. The line from you to the wall represents the path of the center of the sound waves moving from the cricket to the wall; the line from the wall to your friend represents the path along which the center of the sound waves were reflected from the wall. Since both lines meet the wall at the same angle, the sound waves must have been reflected at the same angle at which they struck the wall.

A bat has a "'built-in sonar installation." It sends out sound (dotted line) and receives an echo (broken line), enabling it to tell the distance and location of obstacles and insects.

squeak and chitter as they squabble over places to sleep during the day. Neither the squeaks nor the chittering sounds are the ones used by bats as they hunt insects. If you want to hear the clicking sounds, you can probably do so. On a quiet summer evening, when bats are about, toss tiny pebbles or small wads of wet absorbent cotton gently into the air four or five feet above your head. In this way, you will probably decoy bats to flit near you. As the bats chase your decoy, they will make a faint clicking sound. The clicks are the sounds of lowest pitch of the total sounds the bats are emitting.

But just how do bats use the sounds to **How do bats use sound?** help them locate prey? The method they use is called *echo-location*. As a bat flies about, it continually emits high-pitched sounds. These sounds have a frequency of 5,000 to 120,000 cycles per second. You will remember that one cycle is one complete vibration. The sounds last from 1/1,000 to 1/2,000 of a second, and they are repeated ten to twenty times a second. When these sounds strike an insect, they bounce back to the bat's ears. Then, the bat increases the number of sounds it emits, sending forth as many as 250 sounds per second. Following the path of the echoes, the bat closes in upon its insect prey. The bats' method of echo-location is very much like radar, except that bats use sound waves, while radar uses a kind of radio wave.

The wonderful precision of the bats' echo-location method is made apparent when you consider how faint is the echo that returns to a bat from an insect as small as a mosquito or a gnat — and that at the same time, echoes are also returning to the bat from twigs, leaves, blades of grass and other obstacles. The American brown bat weighs only about one-quarter of an ounce. In a night's hunting, this little bat catches insects whose total weight is equal to its own. Scientists have found that this means the bat catches a mosquito every six seconds, all through the night.

Certain birds also use echo-location. So do animals that live in the sea. Two scientists experimented with a porpoise, one of the animals that locates its prey by echo-location. The scientists found that a porpoise has a vocabulary of grunts, whistles, squeals, clicks and rasping sounds. However, the sound that the porpoise uses for echo-location is a sort of creak. In a muddy pond on a pitch-dark night, the porpoise was able to echo-locate a six-inch fish held in the water by a scientist. This feat is even more remarkable when you know that the part of the fish's body from which the creaks echoed back to the porpoise was the fish's swim-bladder, an air-filled sac only about an inch in diameter.

How does the porpoise use sound to catch fish in the sea?

Perhaps you have seen a blind person walking on a busy street almost as well as a person who can see. It has been known for a long time that some blind persons develop a seemingly new sense to take the place of their lost sight. When questioned about this "sense," blind persons said they could just "feel" or "know" the presence of objects nearby. Some said it was their face, some said it was their forehead, and still others said it was their hands that gave them the feeling that they were near an object.

How do people who are blind locate objects?

In a series of experiments, scientists covered first the face, then the forehead, then the hands and then the ears of each blind person with whom they worked. It was not until the ears were covered that a blind person lost his ability to detect objects in front of himself. Just as in the case of Spallanzani's bats, this experiment proved that hearing is the sense that blind persons substitute for their lost sight. But scientists have not yet learned exactly what sounds blind persons use for echo-location.

When submarines were first used in warfare, anti-submarine ships found themselves confronted with the problem of locating an enemy ship that could remain completely concealed beneath the sea. To solve this problem, scientists developed an underwater electrical echo-locator that was later called *sonar*.

How do ships locate enemy submarines?

At first, sensitive sound-receiving devices were lowered beneath the surface of the ocean, and the anti-submarine ships simply tried to hear the sounds of the submarine. This idea had some success, but the submarine did not always oblige by making distinguishable sounds. Also, the sounds of the listening ship's own engines or the engines of ships being escorted interfered with sounds that might be those of a submarine.

An improved device consisted of both an instrument that could send out powerful sound waves and a sensitive listening instrument. The first instrument sent out a beam of short pulses of sound, and the second instrument picked up any echo that might have resulted from sound pulses striking an underwater obstacle — such as a submarine. Modern sonar sends out sound as powerful as six million loud shouts and can locate a submarine several miles away.

Still another improvement in submarine detection is being developed in the United States — one that may make possible the detection of enemy undersea craft thousands of miles away. The program, known as Project Artemis, makes use of a giant underwater sound generator to convert electric waves into sound waves. Hydrophones are placed at different sea depths to pick up the sound waves from objects in the ocean.

Sonar has found peaceful uses. It is used to determine the depth of water in which ships are moving. Before sonar, depth was found by throwing overboard a weighted line, known as a lead line. At every few feet, the lead line had either a knot or a ring of lead.

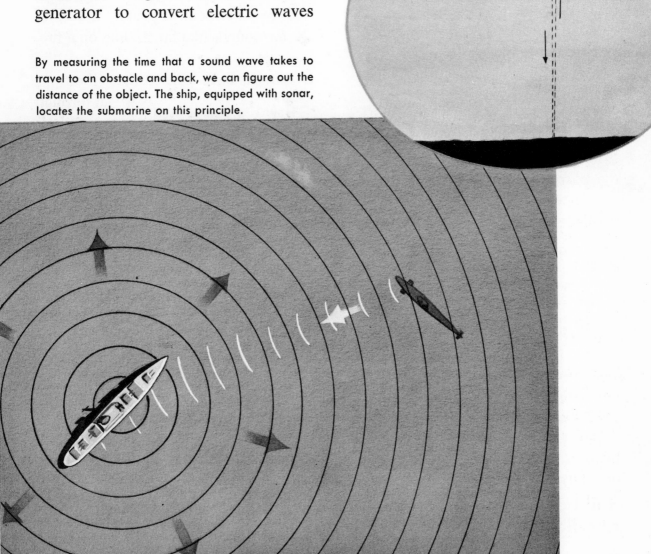

By measuring the time that a sound wave takes to travel to an obstacle and back, we can figure out the distance of the object. The ship, equipped with sonar, locates the submarine on this principle.

When the weight touched bottom, the line was hauled up, the knots or rings were counted and the depth of the water was known from the length of the line that had been underwater. Compare

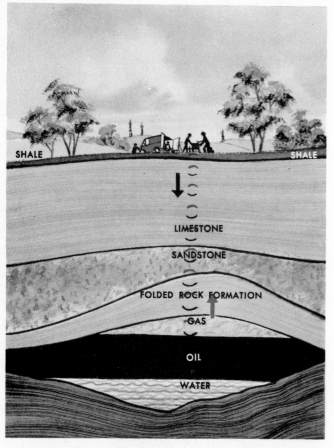

Shown is a cutaway view of an oil deposit in the earth, showing typical echo patterns that enable the geologist to locate the presence of the precious commodity, as well as the best location to drill for it. A seismograph records the echo patterns.

this slow process with sonar. A sound impulse is sent out from the ship's bottom. It strikes the sea bottom and echoes back to the ship. The time taken by the sound impulse's round trip is divided by two — and the depth of the water is known. Since sound travels about 5,000 feet a second in sea water, to find depth by sonar usually takes only a fraction of a second.

Fishermen found that they could use

How are echoes used to detect schools of fish?

sonar to locate schools of fish, for as we have learned, sound is reflected from the swim bladders of fish. When fishermen have determined the location of the school, nets can be cast with accuracy. If you do not send out any sound impulses, you can use sonar simply to listen to underwater sounds.

Sailors listening with sonar have been amazed to learn that the creatures of the sea are not silent as was previously believed. Toadfish make a sound like a base drum, the squirrelfish grinds its teeth to make a sound like a rusty hinge, and certain rockfish grunt. A bed of shrimp sounds like fat sizzling on a fire.

Geologists have learned that vibrations

How are echoes used to locate minerals?

travel through various kinds of rock and soil at varying speeds, and that vibrations are reflected strongly by hard rock and weakly by soft rock and soil. This knowledge gives geologists a method by which to prospect for minerals beneath the surface of the earth without digging. They use an instrument, called a *seismograph,* to record vibrations sent through the earth from small explosions set off in an area. The seismograph tells the travel-time and strength of the vibrations. From this data, geologists can tell through what kinds of rock the vibrations passed and from what kinds they were reflected. They also know what echo patterns indicate the presence of rocks in which oil and many other valuable minerals are found.

Musical Sounds and Musical Instruments

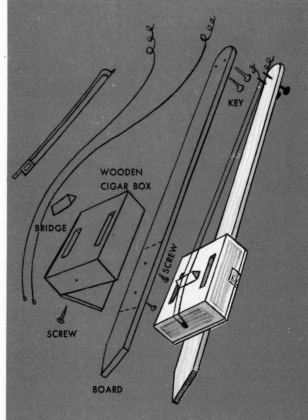

What is musical sound? Most of us would say that music is the sound made by a band, or an orchestra or by a musical instrument. We would say that music is the sound made by a chorus of singers or one person singing alone. We would probably consider music to be the sounds we make when blowing into a tin whistle, or moaning into a kazoo or when singing in the shower or bathtub. In short, we ordinarily consider any pleasing series of sounds to be musical.

A scientist would not deny us our definition of a musical sound, but he would require a more precise definition for his work. He would say that a musical sound is one whose wave pattern is regular; that is, the waves are evenly-spaced and all have the same amplitude. You will remember that amplitude of sound waves is a measure of their loudness. The sound made by a tuning fork is a good example of a musical sound. So is the sound of a siren.

We will better understand a musical sound if we learn what noise is. Ordinarily, we would say that noise is any

HOW YOU CAN MAKE A GUITAR OR A VIOLONCELLO

With a pocket knife, cut two rectangular holes in the bottom of a cigar box. Obtain a board about twenty inches long, two inches wide and three-quarters of an inch thick. Saw out a two-inch section at one end, and fasten the board to the bottom of the box with small bolts. Fasten the lid shut. Whittle two violin pegs, or buy them at a music store. In the middle of the free end of the board, drill holes into which the pegs fit tightly. Whittle a triangular piece of wood for a bridge. Run two guitar strings from screws at the end of the box, over the bridge and to the pegs. Wind the strings tight. Now you can strum tunes on your guitar. If you use a board about four feet long, and fasten the cigar box a foot from one end and use violin strings, you will have a violoncello upon which you can play with a violin bow.

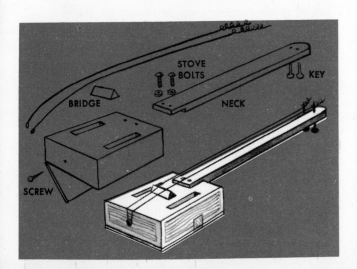

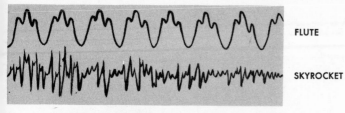

FLUTE

SKYROCKET

Sound waves that show a regular pattern (top) have a pleasing sound, while unpleasant sounds are produced by things that vibrate irregularly.

sound we don't like. For instance, probably everyone dislikes the screech of automobile brakes, and we would call this sound noise. But the sound waves that make up the screech may have a regular pattern. A scientist, then, however much he may dislike the screech, would have to call it a musical sound, according to his definition.

Suppose you are talking on the telephone, while your sister in the same room is practicing her singing lesson. If you have difficulty hearing what is being said to you on the phone, you will consider your sister's singing to be noise, even though every note she sings may be a pure musical sound. Here, again, a common idea about sound conflicts with the scientific definition.

However, we still have to be given a scientific definition of noise. From what we have already learned, you can probably guess that, scientifically, noise is sound made by an irregular pattern of waves. When you stamp your foot on the pavement, drop a book or clap your hands, the sound you make is noise.

Man was making music long before he

What is a musical scale?

began to study it. He sang, stamped and clapped his hands. Probably some prehistoric hunter who found the twang of his

bowstring pleasing, experimented with stretched strings until he invented the first musical instrument. Archaeologists — persons who dig up buried cities to study the civilizations that built them — have found crude lyres that were made by stretching strings of different length across bent tree branches.

The ancient Greeks, who played on lyres and other stringed musical instruments, were the first to study music scientifically. Their musicians established a series of sounds of ascending and descending pitch; that is, a scale of musical notes.

The Greek scientists learned that if a tightly stretched string produces a sound of a certain pitch, then a string half as long produces a sound with a pitch exactly eight notes — called an *octave* — higher on the musical scale. A string half as long as the second one produces a pitch eight more notes higher. In short, they learned that if the length of a vibrating string is halved, its pitch is doubled.

The keys of a piano produce sounds of different pitch. In the musical notes (above) and on the piano (below) is a scale in which the last tone is one octave higher than the first.

DO RE MI FA SO LA TI DO

30

The Greeks also learned that a taut string produces a higher pitch than a loose string, and a thin string produces a higher pitch than a thick one. They did not understand the reasons for all these facts. Since the time of the Greeks, we have learned that pitch depends on frequency. This fact explains what the Greeks learned about vibrating strings. If we measure the frequency of short, tight or thin vibrating strings, we find it is higher than the frequency of long, loose or thick strings.

Any musical sound is made by vibrations twice as fast as those of a sound that is an octave lower, and half as fast as those of a sound that is an octave higher. Middle C has a frequency of 256 cycles per second; the next lower C has a frequency of 128; and the C next higher to middle C has a frequency of 512.

An octave actually includes thirteen tones or musical notes — eight whole notes and five half notes. On a piano the white keys represent whole notes,

the black keys half notes. To move from one white key to the next is to move from one whole note to the next. To move from a white key to a black key, or from black to white, is to move one half note.

What is harmony? When two or more musical notes sounded at the same time produce a pleasing sound, we say they are in *harmony*. When the sound is displeasing, we say the notes are in *discord*. Scientists have discovered that harmony de-

HOW TO MAKE A HARP

Nail three pieces of board together in the form of a triangle. Obtain eight or ten rubber bands, and break each rubber band so that you can pull it out into a single length. Stretch the rubber bands tightly, and fasten them to the sides of the wooden triangle with thumbtacks. You have made a harp on which you can play tunes by plucking the rubber bands. Another way of making a harp is by gluing a right-angled triangle to the bottom of a wooden cigar box, and stringing the rubber bands as shown in the drawing below. Your harp also illustrates that the length and pitch of a vibrating string are related. You will hear that the short rubber bands produce a higher tone than the long ones.

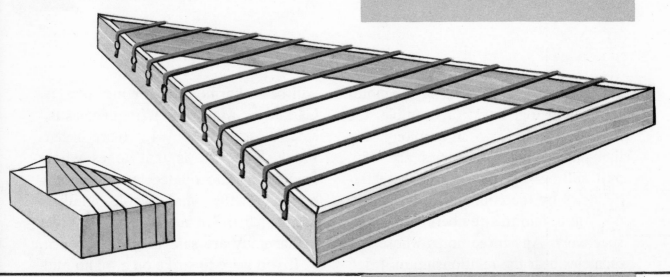

HOW TO MAKE A MILK-BOTTLE ORGAN

You can make an organ from bottles and water. Obtain eight empty soda bottles. Place them in a row. Put a little water in the bottom of the first bottle and a little more water in the second bottle. In the third bottle, put an amount of water that is slightly more than that in the second bottle. Continue to put water in the bottles until the eighth bottle is about two-thirds full. Blow your breath across the top of each bottle in turn. You will see that the more water there is in a bottle, the higher a note it produces. By removing or adding a little water to the bottles, you can make them produce a musical scale. Then, by blowing your breath across their tops, you can play tunes. If you become tired blowing your breath, you can move air across the tops of the bottles by using a vacuum cleaner hose.

HOW TO MAKE A WATER-TROMBONE

To make a trombone, fill a bottle with water to about two inches from the top. A soda bottle will do very well. Put a drinking straw into the bottle. Hold the straw steady with one hand and move the bottle up and down with the other hand, while you blow your breath across the top of the straw. The pitch of the sound emitted by the straw will vary according to how much of the straw is in the water. This is so because the amount of water in the straw determines the length of the vibrating air column above it.

HOW TO MAKE A NAIL-PIANO

Drive eight thin nails into a board in a row, three-quarters of an inch apart. Drive each nail a little farther into the board than the nail preceding it. Push another nail into the end of a cork or a small piece of wood. Use this nail to strike the other nails in the board. The shorter the nail, the higher the pitch of a sound it will produce. You can play tunes on your nail-piano.

HOW TO MAKE A XYLOPHONE

To make a xylophone, you will need eight pieces of hard wood, such as broom handles are made of. Cut the pieces to the following lengths: 10, 9 ½, 9, 8 ¾, 8 ½, 7 ¾, 7 ¼ and 7 inches. Tie the pieces of wood together with strings, as shown. You can play a tune on your xylophone by striking the wooden bars with another stick of hard wood. If you want to tune your xylophone, cut a little off the end of a bar to raise its pitch, or whittle a little from the middle of a bar to lower its tone.

HOW TO MAKE A SLIDE-WHISTLE

You can make a slide-whistle from a piece of bamboo. Cut a notch in the bamboo tube near one end. Whittle a piece of soft wood into the shape of a cylinder, which will fit into the tube. Then, shave off one side of the cylinder to make it flat. Place the cylinder into the tube above the notch. When you blow into this end of the tube, you will hear a whistle as the air goes out of the notch and makes the column of air in the tube vibrate. Whittle another cylinder of soft wood — this one to fit loosely in the tube. Glue the cylinder to the head of a nail or to the eraser of a pencil. Insert the cylinder into the open end of your whistle. By sliding this cylinder up and down the tube, you can change the pitch of your slide-whistle, as you vary the length of the vibrating column of air within the tube.

pends on the frequencies of the notes that sound together. For example, the notes C, E and G are in harmony, and their respective frequencies are 256, 320 and 384. If you divide these frequencies by the common denominator 64, you obtain the numbers 4, 5, 6, respectively. Any three notes whose frequencies bear the relationship of 4:5:6 will be in harmony — for instance, A, C♯ and E. Many other frequencies besides those related by 4:5:6 are in harmony. The rule is that tones whose frequencies are related by any combination of the small whole numbers 1:2:3:4:5:6:7:8 are in harmony. Notes in harmony are said to form a *chord*.

If you were to strike on a piano mid-

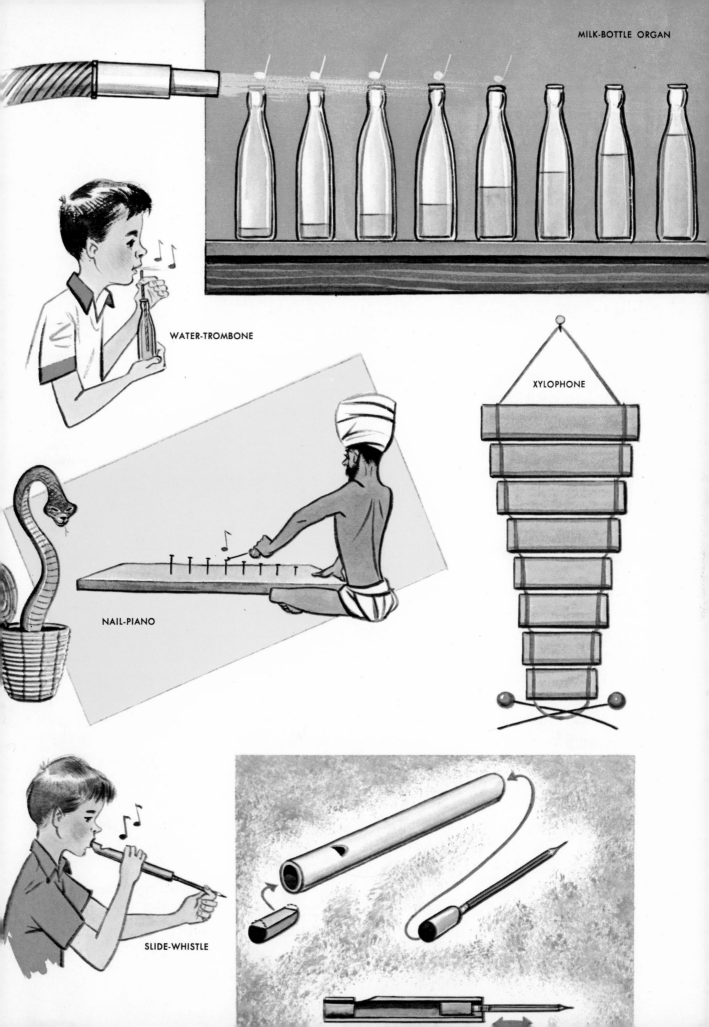

MILK-BOTTLE ORGAN

WATER-TROMBONE

XYLOPHONE

NAIL-PIANO

SLIDE-WHISTLE

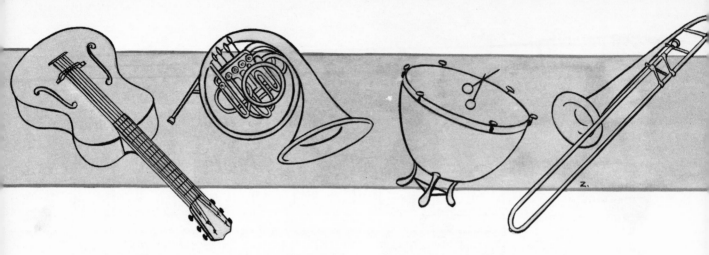

dle C and C♯, the resulting sound would not be pleasant. Keeping in mind what we just learned, we can easily see why these two notes produce discord. Their frequencies are 256 and 271 and are related to each other as 4:4⅕. Since these are not both whole numbers, the sound they produce is a discord.

You probably know of many stringed instruments. The

How do stringed instruments produce sound?

violin, cello, guitar, banjo, zither and harp are some of them. All these instruments consist of two main parts: the strings, and another part that vibrates in resonance with the strings to enrich their sound. For example, the violin is a box of thin wood over which strings are stretched. The strings are made to vibrate by plucking or by drawing a bow over them. The strings vary in tautness and thickness. In the harp and zither the strings are of different lengths. The performer on a stringed instrument can change the pitch of a string by pressing his finger on it, thereby varying the length of the vibrating part of the string.

Thus, by the use of strings of varying length, tautness and thickness, tone of a great variety of pitch may be produced by stringed instruments.

Wind instruments include the trombone, trumpet, bu-

How do wind instruments produce sound?

gle, tuba, flute, piccolo, clarinet and saxophone. A wind instrument is constructed so that blowing breath into it causes a column of air inside to vibrate. The frequency of the vibration depends on the frequency of the air column. The shorter the air column, the higher the frequency, and hence, the higher the pitch of the instrument.

The lengths of vibrating air columns —and consequently the pitch—of wind instruments may be varied by opening and closing holes at different locations. This is the way it is done in the flute, piccolo, clarinet and saxophone. In the trombone, the length of the air column is varied by sliding a U-shaped hollow pipe back and forth; and in the trumpet and French horn, finger valves block parts of the air column to vary its length.

The pitch of a wind instrument also varies according to the width of the vibrating air column. In an organ, the long, wide pipes make low-pitched sounds, and the short, narrow pipes make high-pitched sounds.

A percussion instrument is one that pro-

How do percussion instruments produce sound?

duces a musical sound when struck in a particular manner. A drum, xylophone, triangle, bell and cymbals are all percussion instruments.

Of course, we know how these instruments produce musical sounds, because we have learned how any struck object vibrates and produces sound waves. The resonant vibration of air within a drum amplifies the sound made by the vibrating drumhead. A piano is a combination of percussion and stringed instruments. Striking a piano key causes a felt hammer to strike strings of different lengths within the piano.

Living Sound Organs

One of the most remarkable instru-

What is the human voice?

ments is the human voice. Its variation in quality is greater than that of any musical instrument. Voice sounds are produced by the vibration of two ligaments, called the *vocal cords*. They are stretched across the larynx (or "Adam's apple") in such a manner as to leave only a narrow slit between them for the passage of air. Air from the lungs passes through the narrow slit and causes the vocal cords to vibrate.

Muscles attached to the vocal cords may increase their pull on the ligaments, thereby tightening and thinning them; or else they may relax their tension, thereby loosening and thickening the ligaments.

We have learned that a tight, thin cord has a higher pitch than a loose, thick one. This principle holds for vocal cords, too. When the vocal cords are tight and thin, the voice is high; when the vocal cords are loose and thick, the voice is low. We also learned that a

Cut a wide rubber band into two equal lengths. Place the two pieces side by side, and grip them firmly between the thumb and forefinger of each hand. Stretch them tight. Touch your lips with the stretched rubber bands, and blow your breath through them. The sound they produce is due to their vibration. You can vary the pitch of this sound by the degree to which you stretch the rubber bands. The rubber bands produce sound in much the same way that your vocal cords do. Muscles stretch the vocal cords to change the pitch of your voice.

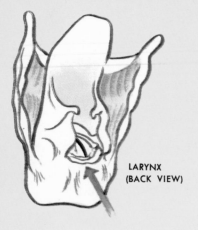

LARYNX
(BACK VIEW)

BULLFROG

KATYDID

VOCAL CORDS
DURING
BREATHING

VOCAL CORDS
DURING
SPEAKING

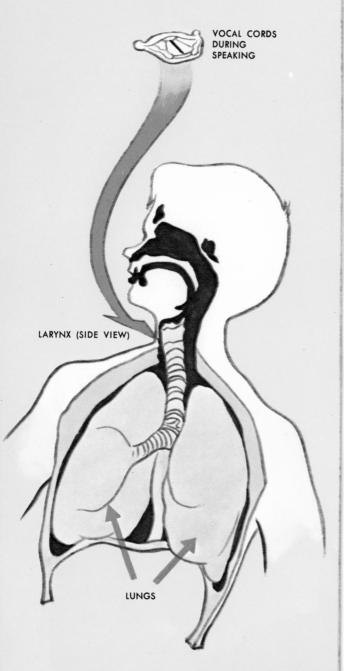

LARYNX (SIDE VIEW)

LUNGS

short vibrating cord has a higher pitch than a long one. So, we should not be surprised to learn that the vocal cords of women are about one-half inch long and those of men are about three-quarters of an inch long. Now you know why the voices of babies are so high — because they have very short vocal cords.

The range between the lowest and highest pitch of the same set of vocal cords is about two-and-a-half octaves.

Of course, vocal cords do not simply make sounds by themselves. They are attached to muscles that enable the owner of the vocal cords to control their actions at will.

The quality of the voice depends upon the manner in which its tones are modified by resonating the cavities of the mouth and nose. You can easily prove this by holding your nostrils closed while you are talking. Note the thinness of your voice. Then remove your fingers and note how much richer your voice is. Also ask a friend to do the same, so that you can hear how resonance increases the richness of his voice.

All the sounds of our speech are not

The human voice organs are the most versatile "sound instruments" in the world.

BIRD

BEE

Although very many kinds of animals make sounds, not all have vocal cords. The dog's bark, the cow's moo, the cat's meow and the sounds of other mammals are made by means of vocal cords. Birds sing, squawk, peep, whistle and chatter by means of a ring of cartilage, called a syrinx, in the bird's windpipe. A male katydid has a file-like row of ridges on one of its wings. When the katydid rubs part of the other wing against this file, sounds are produced that seem to say ''katy-did, katy-did,'' or ''she didn't, she didn't.'' A bee's hum is made by the rapid motion of its wings, causing the surrounding air to vibrate. To increase the loudness of its croaks, a bullfrog may puff up its throat like a balloon. The distended throat acts as a resonator that magnifies the sound made by the frog's vocal cords.

made by our vocal cords. For example, when we say a word that contains the letter *t*, we make a slight clicking sound by suddenly pulling the tongue away from the roof of the mouth just behind the front teeth. To make *b* and *p* sounds, we cause an explosion of air through our lips. The *s* is a hissing sound.

Although musical instruments may have a greater range, none has the capability of expression of the human voice. A voice may be soft, harsh, nasal, throaty; friendly, angry, commanding, cajoling, whining; and have a hundred other shades, meanings and qualities.

Everyone knows we hear with our ears.

How do we hear? But it is worthwhile to understand how these wonderful organs work. The human ear may be divided into three main parts: the *outer ear,* the *middle ear* and the *inner ear.* The outer ear consists of the part on the outside of the head (made of cartilage), and also the *auditory canal.* The cartilaginous part of the ear helps to direct sound waves into the auditory canal, a passageway through which sounds reach

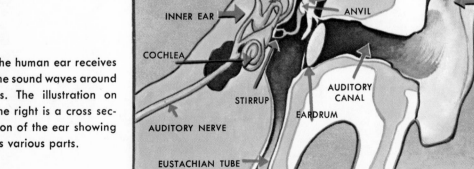

The human ear receives the sound waves around us. The illustration on the right is a cross section of the ear showing its various parts.

SEMICIRCULAR CANALS
MIDDLE EAR
HAMMER
ANVIL
OUTER EAR
INNER EAR
COCHLEA
STIRRUP
AUDITORY CANAL
EARDRUM
AUDITORY NERVE
EUSTACHIAN TUBE

the middle ear. Stretching across the inner end of the auditory canal and completely blocking it is a circular membrane, the *eardrum*. Inward from the eardrum is the middle ear.

Touching the inner surface of the eardrum is a tiny bone, the *malleus*, or hammer. The malleus connects by a joint to another little bone, the *incus*, or anvil. And the incus is joined to a third little bone, the *stapes*, or stirrup — so named because it looks like a stirrup. These three bones stretch across the cavity of the middle ear, from front to back. The lower part of the middle ear opens upon the *Eustachian tube* that leads to the throat. Because of this tube, air pressure in the middle ear can be equalized with air pressure outside the eardrum.

The stapes touches a snail-shaped tube called the *cochlea*. The cochlea opens upon three thin tubes, the *semicircular canals*. Both the cochlea and the semicircular canals are filled with liquid. Inward from the cochlea, the *auditory nerve* leads to the brain.

When sound waves strike the eardrum and cause it to vibrate, the eardrum causes the malleus to vibrate, too.

The malleus strikes against the incus with each vibration. The incus passes the vibration to the stapes. These three tiny bones serve to multiply by more than twenty times the strength of vibrations of the eardrum.

The footplate of the stapes passes the vibrations to the liquid in the inner ear. Here, the vibrations press upon certain tissues, called *organs of Corti*. These organs change the pressure into nerve impulses that are carried to the brain by the auditory nerve. The brain interprets the impulses as sound.

This complicated system works very well. It can make you aware of a very wide range and complex combination of sound, such as that which reaches your ear from an orchestra. The ear can transmit vibrations to the brain having frequencies of from 20 cycles to 20,000 cycles per second. Children may be able to hear sound of more than 30,000 cycles per second. At 2,000 cycles per second, the human ear may be able to hear sounds so faint that they have an amplitude of less than 1/500,000,000 of an inch — about one-half the diameter of the hydrogen atom, the smallest of all atoms.

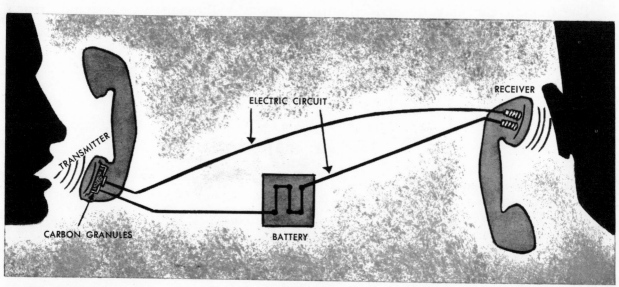

ELECTRIC CIRCUIT

RECEIVER

TRANSMITTER

CARBON GRANULES

BATTERY

Sound and Communication

A telephone does not really carry sound.

How does a telephone carry sound? How, then, can a person at one end of a telephone line hear voices, music or any other sound made at the other end? A telephone has two main parts. One is the *mouthpiece,* or *transmitter,* and the other is the *receiver.* You speak into the transmitter and hold the receiver to your ear.

Inside the transmitter is a small round box filled with grains of carbon. The top of this box is a thin metal disk, called a *diaphragm.* When you talk into the transmitter, the sound waves produced by your voice cause the diaphragm to vibrate. The back-and-forth movements of the diaphragm alternately press the carbon grains together and then leave them room to spread apart.

There is an electric circuit in the telephone wires that runs between your phone and the phone of the person to whom you are talking. When the diaphragm presses the carbon grains together, more electric current flows in the circuit; when the grains are farther apart, less current flows. Thus, the amount of electric current in a telephone circuit varies from moment to moment as the diaphragm vibrates.

In the receiver is another diaphragm. This diaphragm rests on a magnet. The strength with which this magnet pulls on the diaphragm varies in proportion to the amount of electric current. When the pull is strong, the diaphragm moves toward the magnet, and when the pull is weak, the diaphragm springs away from the magnet. The back-and-forth movements of the diaphragm generate air waves that reach your ear as sound. Because the vibrations of the diaphragm in the transmitter control the flow of current, they produce identical vibrations of the diaphragm in the receiver. Thus, the sound waves that leave the receiver are identical with those that enter the transmitter. As a result, you can hear sound coming from the receiver just as though the sound had traveled along the wire.

A microphone in a broadcasting studio is constructed very much like a transmitter of a telephone.

How does a radio transmit sound without wires? Sound waves entering the microphone cause it to vary electrical impulses. These impulses, instead of flowing

At left is a cutaway view of the handpiece of a modern telephone, showing the principal parts of the transmitter and receiver. The diagram next to it shows a simple telephone circuit with a battery. (After diagrams, courtesy Bell Telephone Laboratories.)

MAGNET

CARBON GRANULES

DIAPHRAGM

COILS

RECEIVER

DIAPHRAGM

TRANSMITTER

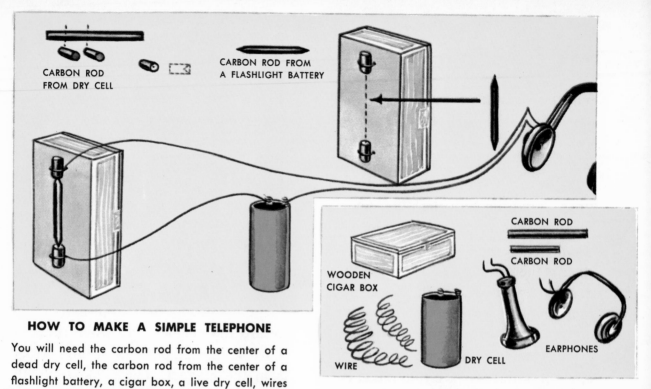

CARBON ROD FROM DRY CELL

CARBON ROD FROM A FLASHLIGHT BATTERY

WOODEN CIGAR BOX

WIRE

DRY CELL

CARBON ROD

CARBON ROD

EARPHONES

HOW TO MAKE A SIMPLE TELEPHONE

You will need the carbon rod from the center of a dead dry cell, the carbon rod from the center of a flashlight battery, a cigar box, a live dry cell, wires and an old telephone receiver or a set of earphones. Saw off two one-inch lengths of the carbon rod from the dead dry cell, and grind out a small hollow in the end of each piece. With sandpaper, sharpen the ends of the rod from the flashlight battery. Affix the two hollowed-out pieces of carbon to the back of the cigar box, using wire in the manner shown. The sharpened carbon rod should be placed between the two pieces of carbon, so that its points touch the hollowed-out place in each piece. Fasten a long piece of bell wire to each of the hollowed-out pieces of carbon, and run one wire to one pole of the live dry cell. Run the other wire to another room, where you connect it to the telephone receiver or headphones. Take a third wire and connect the other pole of the dry cell with the receiver, as the illustration shows. Your telephone is complete. If someone talks into the front of the cigar box, the movement of the sharpened carbon rod will vary the amount of electric current in the wires, and the diaphragm of the receiver will vibrate to produce the same sound waves as those of the person speaking into the box.

through wires to a receiver, go to electronic equipment that transforms them into electromagnetic, or radio, waves. These waves are broadcast. When the waves reach a radio, other electronic devices change the radio waves to electrical impulses. These impulses are transformed into sound waves by the radio's speaker, which works on the same principle as a telephone receiver.

Not very long ago, a famous speech, a

How can we record sound?

brilliant performance by a musician or the clever words of a little child could be heard once — and

then were lost to our ears forever. Of course, you know that nowadays we can hear over and over again any sounds we choose — if we record them in any of several ways. But how do we go about recording sounds? In 1877, the American inventor Thomas Alva Edison wrapped tin foil about a wooden cylinder. The cylinder was arranged so that it could be turned by a crank attached to one end. Edison also attached a needle to one side of a metal diaphragm and rested the needle on the tin-foil cylinder. The other side of the diaphragm rested on a large horn.

While Edison turned the crank, he

shouted into the horn, "Mary had a little lamb!" The sound waves of his voice made the diaphragm vibrate. The diaphragm moved the attached needle up and down and cut grooves into the tin foil.

When Edison had finished his recitation, he put the needle at the beginning of the grooves and again turned the crank. Now, the needle bumped along the same grooves and the diaphragm vibrated, producing sound waves. As a result, the first phonograph repeated in a faint, tinny voice, "Mary had a little lamb."

Within ten years, tin-foil cylinders had been replaced by wax cylinders, and these, in turn, had given way to flat disks, such as we use today. Also, a way had been found to cut grooves in sidewise zigzags, instead of up-and-down bumps.

In the 1920's electronic principles were applied to phonograph recording. This is the method used today. Sound enters a microphone and is changed into electrical impulses. These impulses vary the strength of a magnet that controls the disk-cutting needle. The disk that is cut by the recording needle is called the master disk. It is electrically covered with a thin coating of metal, and it is used as a mold from which to make many other disks.

Put a record on a turntable and start the phonograph running. Place your fingernail lightly on the grooves of the record. You will hear sound coming from your fingernail, and you will also feel the sound as the vibrations produced by the motion of your fingernail are transmitted along the bones of your arm.

With a magnifying glass, examine the grooves in a phonograph record. Note how they wiggle back and forth. As the disk turns, the phonograph needle runs along the groove, wiggling back and forth as it follows the turnings and twistings of the groove.

Push a needle through a corner of a clean milk carton. Hold the needle in the grooves of a record turning on a turntable. You will find that the carton acts as a resonator that magnifies the vibrations of the needle, so that you can hear sound coming from the record. Use caution to avoid damage to the record.

41

Electronic equipment is also used to cause the phonograph disk to reproduce sound from the zigzags cut in it. The phonograph needle is attached to a device much like a telephone transmitter. The zigzag motion of the needle, as the grooves run beneath it, is changed into electrical impulses. These varying impulses vary the strength of a magnet in a speaker, and sound issues from the speaker, just as it does in a radio.

Our two ears cause us to hear sound

What is stereophonic sound?

more richly and vividly than if we had just one ear. Two ears give sound a quality of direction and depth. You can easily prove this by holding a hand tightly over one ear while you listen to any sounds, perhaps music. You will find that music heard through one ear lacks a feeling of depth and is less vivid than the same music heard through both ears.

If only one microphone is used to make a recording, it is similar to listening with one ear. If, on the other hand, separate microphones are used to record sounds that come from the right and from the left, the situation is similar to listening with two ears. When two microphones are used, the needle cuts a separate set of zigzags in each side of the groove it is making — one set for the sound coming to each microphone.

When a disk recorded in this manner is played on a phonograph, the needle reproduces sound separately from the zigzags on each side of the groove. The electrical impulses generated in this way flow to two speakers, each speaker receiving impulses from one side of the groove. The resulting sound has a quality of depth, so that you feel as though you were in the room in which the sound was recorded.

In a wire recorder, we again use a micro

How does a wire or tape recorder work?

phone to change sound waves to varying electrical impulses; and, again, the impulses vary the strength of a magnet. Moving past the magnet is a wire that unwinds from one reel and winds on another, as the reels are turned by an electric motor. The moving wire is magnetized, and the amount of magnetization on any part of the wire depends on the strength of the magnet at the moment the wire passed it. In this way, sound waves are translated into lengths of wire, magnetized to varying strengths.

In order to take sound off the magnetized wire, the wire is rewound on the original reel, and then, by means of switches in the recorder, a new electrical circuit is set up. Now, as the wire moves past the magnet, the wire's vary-

ing magnetic strength causes electrical impulses to vary the strength of a magnet in a speaker. The speaker changes the varying strength of the magnet into sound, just as it does in a telephone receiver, or a radio or phonograph speaker.

A tape recorder works the same way as a wire recorder, but instead of a wire, it uses a tape made of two plastic ribbons. Sandwiched between the ribbons is powdered iron, a metal that is very easily magnetized.

Tape recorders also have medical uses. Doctors may record heart beats on tape recorders, and then they can listen to their patients' heart beats at any time. These tapes are kept as part of the medical record.

How are sound movies made?

In making sound movies, we once again use a microphone to change sound waves into electrical impulses. This time, the varying electrical impulses vary the brightness of a light bulb. A strip on one side of the film moves past the light bulb at the same time that the action is being photographed on the film. When the film is developed, the strip on the side bears varying light and dark areas. They are due to the varying amount of light that reached the film from the light bulb. On a phonograph record, sound is represented by the zigzag grooves; on a tape recorder, sound is represented by lengths of different magnetization; and on a sound-movie film, sound is represented by light and dark areas on a strip at one side. This strip is called the *sound track*.

When a sound movie is projected, the sound track moves past a light bulb whose light shines through the film. The light and dark areas on the sound track vary the amount of light that passes through the film. The varying light strikes an electronic device that changes light into electrical impulses. The electrical impulses, of varying strength, enter a speaker and are changed into sound waves.

Thus, as the picture of people or things photographed on the film is projected on a screen, the sounds made at the time of photographing come from the speaker at the same time. In this way, the voice of an actor, who was speaking when he was photographed, can be heard as we see him move about the movie screen.

The sound track of a movie is synchronized with pictures on the same film.

Ultrasonics and Supersonics

Ultrasonics concerns sound waves —

What is ultrasonics? or more accurately, longitudinal waves — that have a frequency higher than what we ordinarily consider to be the highest frequency of sound waves. Ultrasonic waves are usually considered to begin at 20,000 cycles per second. This, as we have learned, is the upper limit for hearing for most human beings, but, as we also know, children can hear sounds of more than 30,000 cycles per second. So, the 20,000-cycle limit for ultrasonic waves is really not an accurate one. Ultrasonic vibrations of more than a million cycles per second have been produced.

Have you ever seen the dog whistles that you cannot hear? When one of these whistles is blown, no sound seems to come from it. The whistle produces ultrasonic waves that a human being cannot hear, but which a dog can hear. Many other animals hear vibrations that are ultrasonic to human beings. For instance, bats can hear vibrations as high as 145,000 cycles per second.

By causing ultrasonic vibrations to pass

How can you wash dishes with sound? through water in which there are dirty dishes, the particles of food can literally be shaken right off the dishes. There

Scientists have studied shock-wave patterns and plane speeds in special wind tunnels, and thus, have helped to develop better planes.

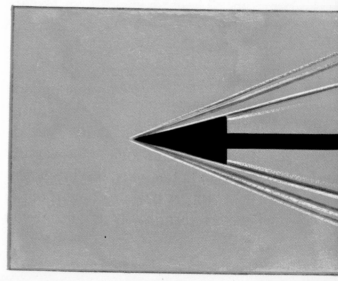

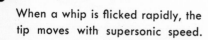

When a whip is flicked rapidly, the tip moves with supersonic speed.

are dishwashers that work this way. Dried blood and other matter are cleaned from surgical and dental instruments by means of ultrasonic vibrations.

What is the sound barrier? When any object moves faster than sound in air, we say that the object is moving with *super-sonic* speed. To move through air with supersonic speed requires a great amount of energy. Let us take an airplane for an example. As the plane moves, it pushes air ahead of itself in a series of waves. You probably have seen water waves being pushed forward and outward from the bow of a boat moving through water. Similar waves of air move ahead and outward from the nose of a plane. As the plane flies faster and faster, it catches up with its nose waves and pushes each wave against the one ahead of it. This results in a gathering of compressed air ahead of the plane. Two waves produce twice as much compression as one wave, and ten waves produce ten times as much. To push this mass of compressed air ahead

of itself, the plane requires a great amount of energy. At the speed of sound — 1,100 feet per second, or 750 miles per hour — the wall of air being pushed before the plane is called the *sound barrier*.

What is a sonic boom? Needle-nose jet and rocket planes are sufficiently powerful to reach, and pass through, the sound barrier. At 750 miles per hour, the nose waves of an airplane, having reached the speed of sound, suddenly become sound waves. At this moment, the powerful compression wave that moves outward from the plane's nose can be heard as a loud explosive sound, called the *sonic boom*.

Soldiers serving in rifle-range target pits hear the loud crack of bullets passing over the pits. This sound is made by the nose waves of the bullets, which are traveling considerably faster than sound. When a whip is flicked rapidly, its tip moves with supersonic speed, and the compression wave in front of the tip is heard as a loud crack.

When an airplane is traveling at less than the speed of sound, it compresses the air in front of it. At 750 miles per hour, the nose waves of an airplane suddenly become sound waves. These waves cause the sonic boom, which often sounds like a heavy explosion in the sky.

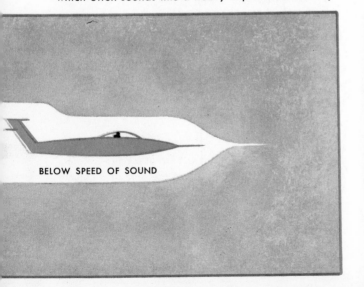

BELOW SPEED OF SOUND

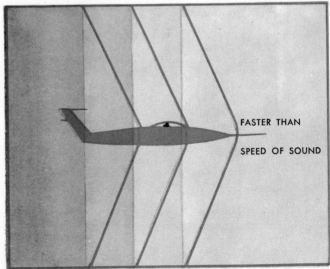

FASTER THAN

SPEED OF SOUND

Some Interesting Facts About Sound

You have learned enough about sound to answer the following questions. Try to answer them before you read the answers.

It is not unusual for soldiers marching in a long column to be out of step. This is likely to be true when soldiers are marching in time to the music of a band at the head of the column. Can you tell why the soldiers at the rear are out of step? We learned that it takes time for sound waves to travel through air. The music of the band reaches the soldiers at the rear of the column after it is heard by the soldiers leading the column. If the column is about 600 feet long, the soldiers at the rear will be a whole pace out of step with those who are leading.

Why are soldiers at the rear of a column sometimes out of step?

Have you ever noticed that the horn of an approaching car seems to have a pitch that is higher than usual. You probably noticed this most clearly just as the automobile reached you, for at that moment, the pitch of the horn suddenly dropped to a much lower note. As sound waves move outward from the horn, waves that are moving in the same direction as the automobile will reach anyone standing to the front of the automobile with the normal speed of sound — *plus* the speed of the vehicle. As a result, if you stand to the front of the automobile, more than the normal number of sound waves reach you per second. This has the same effect as increasing the frequency of the sound, because frequency is measured in waves

Why does an approaching automobile horn have a higher pitch than usual?

While marching to the beat of a band, soldiers at the rear of a column are often out of step. Can you explain why this happens?

(or cycles) per second. Now, we have learned that an increase in frequency results in an increase in pitch. Thus, the horn of an approaching automobile seems to increase in pitch.

At the moment the automobile passes

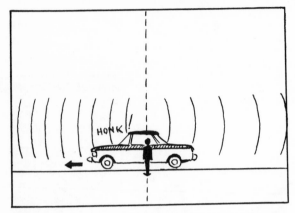

As a train moves away from you, fewer sound waves reach your ear per second than when the train approaches you. This causes the seeming drop in pitch as the train speeds by.

you, the sound waves now moving sidewise from the horn have only their usual speed. Thus, the frequency is lower and so is the pitch.

After the automobile has passed you, the sound waves reach you with the normal speed of sound — *minus* the speed of the automobile. Fewer sound waves reach you per second. This is the same as lessening the frequency — and consequently, lowering the pitch of the sound.

The seeming change in the pitch of a moving sound is called the *Doppler Effect*. The reason for the seeming change was first given by an Austrian physicist, Christian Johann Doppler, in 1842. While walking with his little daughter, he heard the seeming change in pitch of a train whistle, and this prompted him to think about the reason for it.

Why is it easier to hear sounds from a boat during the day than at nighttime?

On a sunny day, people at the beach are sometimes surprised to find how well they can hear sounds coming from boats not very far offshore. And at night, people in boats near the shore can hear sounds from land quite clearly. Why is this so? On a sunny day, the sun heats the surface of the land faster than the surface of water. The air over the land is warmed quickly and it rises. The place of this air is taken by cooler air flowing in from over the water. This air carries with it the sounds

At the beach, it is easier to hear sounds coming from a boat during the day than at night. But on a boat, it is easier to hear sounds coming from the beach at night than during the day.

that were made over the surface of the water — on boats, for instance.

At night, the surface of the water is warmer than the surface of the land. This reverses the flow of air, so that it goes from land to water. Thus, sounds on land are carried out to persons who are in boats.

You can hear the "sound of the sea" in a sea shell only when other sounds cause the shell to resonate.

Once there was a man who found a large sea shell on the shore. He put it to his ear and heard

When can you hear the "sound of the sea" in a shell?

what seemed to be the sound of the sea coming from the shell. He decided to take it home to his children. While he was driving home, he was stopped for a while in traffic. He put the sea shell to his ear and was pleased to hear the "sound of the sea" quite clearly.

When he reached home, he showed his children what he had found. Wanting them to hear the sounds in the shell as clearly as possible, he took his children into a quiet room. But when the children put the sea shell to their ears, they could hardly hear anything. What had happened?

When the man held the sea shell to his ear on the beach, the shell acted as a resonator for the sounds of the waves breaking in the surf. The noises of traffic, too, caused the shell to resonate and to produce a sighing sound of varying strength, much like the sound of the sea. In the quiet room, however, there was little continual sound to make the shell resonate.

You have learned much about sound.

Your new world of sound . . .

The many sounds that you hear all day long can take on a new meaning, now that you understand how and why they are made and act as they do. This scientific knowledge should increase your interest in the world of sound that is around you.

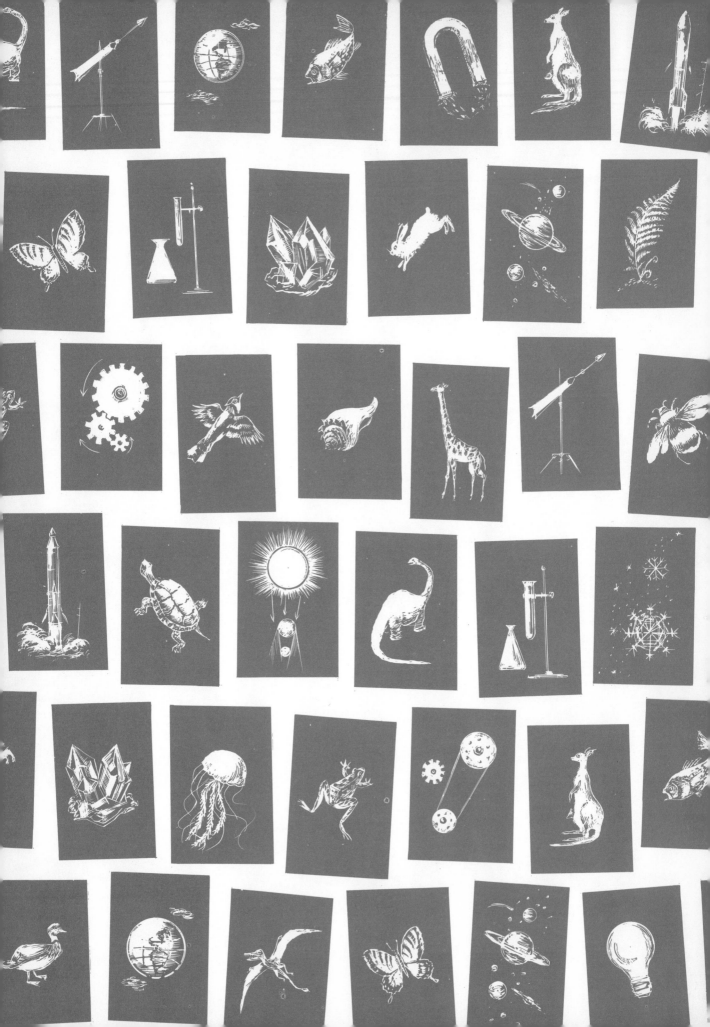